There Was a Man Who Loved a Rat

AND OTHER VILE LITTLE POEMS

WRITTEN BY

Gerda Rovetch

ILLUSTRATED BY

Lissa Rovetch

PHILOMEL BOOKS

PHILOMEL BOOKS

A division of Penguin Young Readers Group.

Published by The Penguin Group.

Penguin Group (USA) Inc., 375 Hudson Street, New York, NY 10014, U.S.A.

Penguin Group (Canada), 90 Eglinton Avenue East, Suite 700, Toronto, Ontario M4P 2Y3, Canada (a division of Pearson Penguin Canada Inc.). Penguin Books Ltd, 80 Strand, London WC2R 0RL, England. Penguin Ireland, 25 St. Stephen's Green, Dublin 2, Ireland (a division of Penguin Books Ltd). Penguin Group (Australia), 250 Camberwell Road, Camberwell, Victoria 3124, Australia (a division of Pearson Australia Group Pty Ltd). Penguin Books India Pvt Ltd, 11 Community Centre, Panchsheel Park, New Delhi - 110 017, India. Penguin Group (NZ), 67 Apollo Drive, Rosedale, North Shore 0745, Auckland, New Zealand (a division of Pearson New Zealand Ltd.). Penguin Books (South Africa) (Pty) Ltd, 24 Sturdee Avenue, Rosebank, Johannesburg 2196, South Africa. Penguin Books Ltd, Registered Offices: 80 Strand, London WC2R 0RL, England.

Published simultaneously in Canada. Manufactured in China by South China Printing Co. Ltd.

Design by Richard Amari.

The illustrations for this book were drawn on paper plates with ink.

The text is set in Kosmik.

Library of Congress Cataloging-in-Publication Data

Rovetch, Gerda.

There was a man who loved a rat and other terrible little poems / Gerda Rovetch ; illustrated by Lissa Rovetch.

p. cm. 1. Children's poetry, American. I. Rovetch, Lissa ill. II. Title. PS3618.087245T47 2008

811.6—dc22   2007023644

ISBN 978-0-399-25014-9

1 3 5 7 9 10 8 6 4 2

There was a man in Abilene

who loved a little lima bean.

He kept it in a velvet bag

and only took it out to brag.

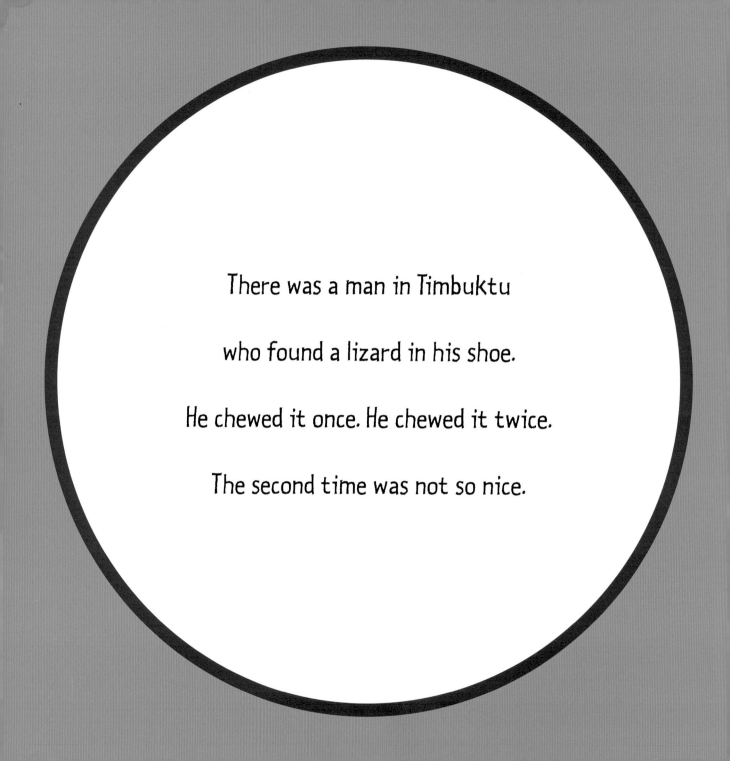

There was a man in Timbuktu

who found a lizard in his shoe.

He chewed it once. He chewed it twice.

The second time was not so nice.

As I was walking on the heath,

I met a man with many teeth.

He showed them to me one by one—

I thought that was a lot of fun.

There was a man who loved sardines.

He always kept some in his jeans.

And when some slipped down on the floor—

that man would just stuff in some more.

A man who dined in Guadeloupe

found a live chicken in his soup.

"So sorry, sir," the waiter said.

"I couldn't find one that was dead."

There was a man who loved a prune.

He cherished it and named it June—

until, one fateful autumn night,

his girlfriend ate it in one bite.

There was a man who loved a starling.

He called it sweetheart, babe, and darling.

It made his wife so sick at heart,

she shot that starling with a dart.

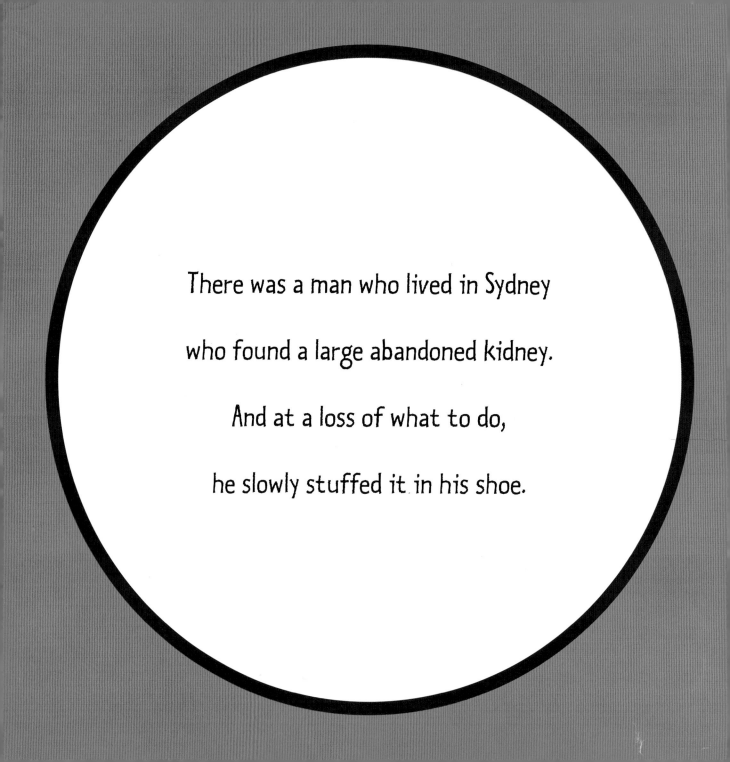

There was a man who lived in Sydney

who found a large abandoned kidney.

And at a loss of what to do,

he slowly stuffed it in his shoe.

There was a man who loved a rat.

He fed it ham till it got fat.

He kept it in his bed at night,

and rather hoped it wouldn't bite.

My uncle found a fine fat worm.

He squeezed it hard and made it squirm.

And though my uncle meant no harm,

that worm eyed him with great alarm.

There was a cunning little mobster

who kept a large and lively lobster.

He aimed the beast at people's ears,

and some remembered it for years.

There was a man who loved a chicken,

and fearful that the bird might sicken,

he kept it in a plastic cube,

and fed the chicken through a tube.

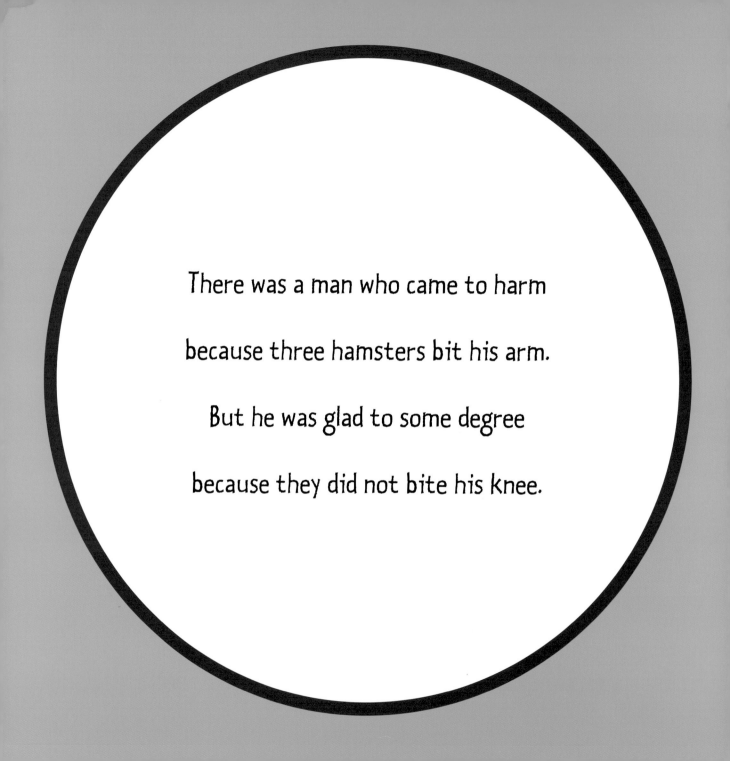

There was a man who came to harm

because three hamsters bit his arm.

But he was glad to some degree

because they did not bite his knee.

There was a man who loved to bake.

Sometimes his bread contained a snake.

Sometimes the snake was not quite dead.

Most people did not like his bread.